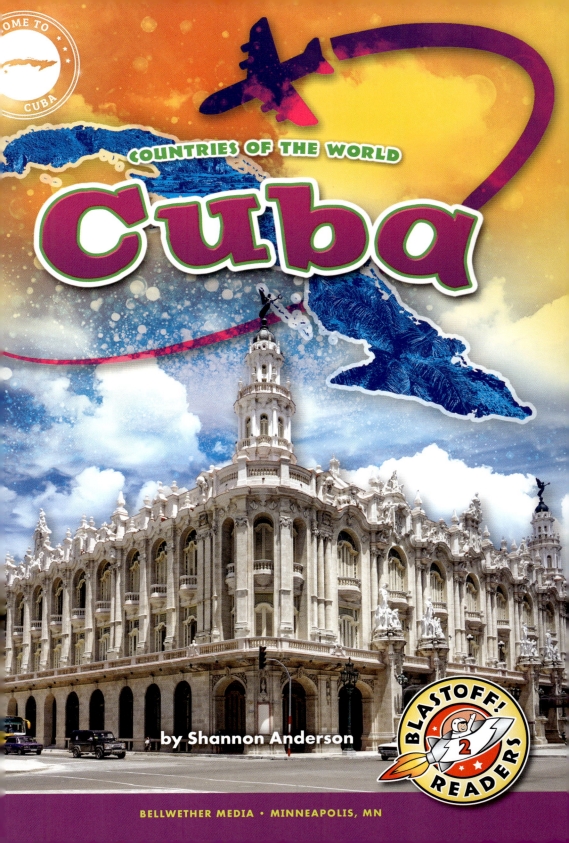

Blastoff! Readers are carefully developed by literacy experts to build reading stamina and move students toward fluency by combining standards-based content with developmentally appropriate text.

Level 1 provides the most support through repetition of high-frequency words, light text, predictable sentence patterns, and strong visual support.

Level 2 offers early readers a bit more challenge through varied sentences, increased text load, and text-supportive special features.

Level 3 advances early-fluent readers toward fluency through increased text load, less reliance on photos, advancing concepts, longer sentences, and more complex special features.

★ **Blastoff! Universe**

This edition first published in 2024 by Bellwether Media, Inc.

No part of this publication may be reproduced in whole or in part without written permission of the publisher. For information regarding permission, write to Bellwether Media, Inc., Attention: Permissions Department, 6012 Blue Circle Drive, Minnetonka, MN 55343.

Library of Congress Cataloging-in-Publication Data

Names: Anderson, Shannon, 1972- author.
Title: Cuba / by Shannon Anderson.
Description: Minneapolis, MN : Bellwether Media, Inc., 2024. | Series: Blastoff! Readers : countries of the world | Includes bibliographical references and index. | Audience: Ages 5-8 | Audience: Grades 2-3 | Summary: "Relevant images match informative text in this introduction to Cuba. Intended for students in kindergarten through third grade"– Provided by publisher.
Identifiers: LCCN 2023003623 (print) | LCCN 2023003624 (ebook) | ISBN 9798886874297 (library binding) | ISBN 9798886876178 (ebook)
Subjects: LCSH: Cuba–Juvenile literature.
Classification: LCC F1758.5 .A53 2024 (print) | LCC F1758.5 (ebook) | DDC 972.91–dc23/eng/20230126
LC record available at https://lccn.loc.gov/2023003623
LC ebook record available at https://lccn.loc.gov/2023003624

Text copyright © 2024 by Bellwether Media, Inc. BLASTOFF! READERS and associated logos are trademarks and/or registered trademarks of Bellwether Media, Inc.

Editor: Rebecca Sabelko   Designer: Gabriel Hilger

Printed in the United States of America, North Mankato, MN.

Table of Contents

All About Cuba	4
Land and Animals	6
Life in Cuba	12
Cuba Facts	20
Glossary	22
To Learn More	23
Index	24

All About Cuba

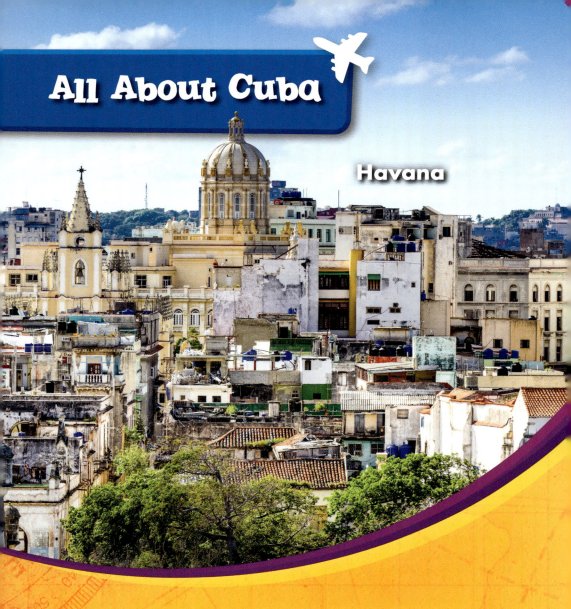

Havana

Cuba is the biggest island in the **West Indies**. It touches the Gulf of Mexico, the Atlantic Ocean, and the Caribbean Sea.

Land and Animals

Most of Cuba is covered in **plains**. Sandy beaches and **mangrove swamps** line the coast. **Coral reefs** lie offshore.

The Sierra Maestra mountains line the southeast.

coral reef

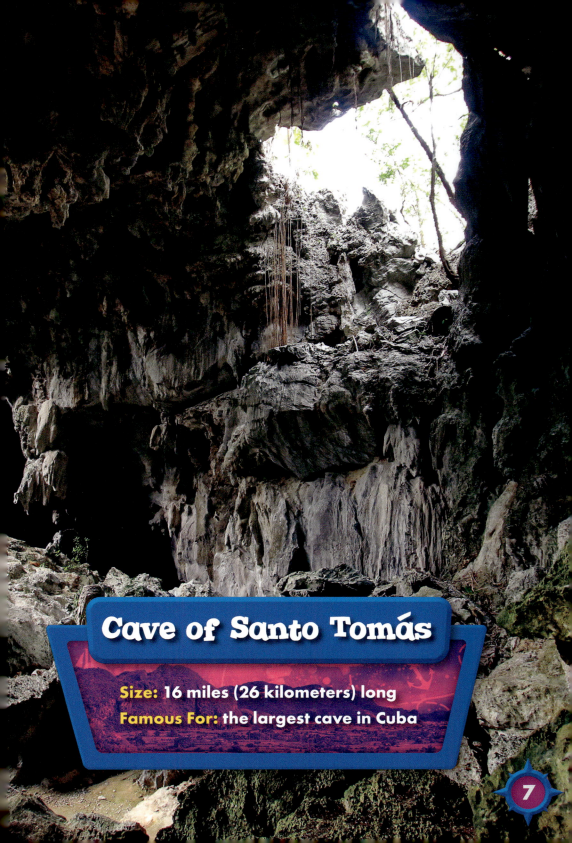

Cave of Santo Tomás

Size: 16 miles (26 kilometers) long
Famous For: the largest cave in Cuba

Cuba is a **tropical** country. Winters are cooler and drier than summers.

Hurricanes are common. They bring dangerous winds and rain in summer.

hurricane

Manatees swim in Cuba's rivers. Iguanas rest in the sun. Bats hang in caves.

Cuban ground iguana

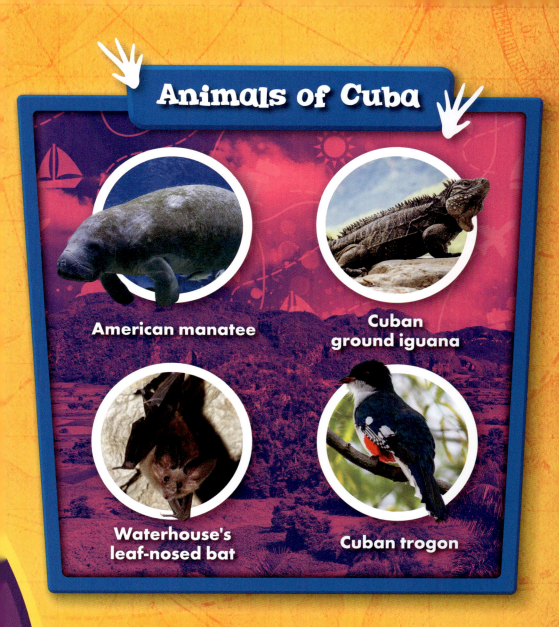

The national bird is the trogon. It is red, white, and blue.

Life in Cuba

Most people have a Spanish background. Some have African **ancestors**.

Spanish is the main language. Over half of the people in Cuba are **Christians**.

museum

Cuba has many libraries and museums. Music and dance are popular.

Baseball is the top sport. Dominoes is a game enjoyed by children and adults.

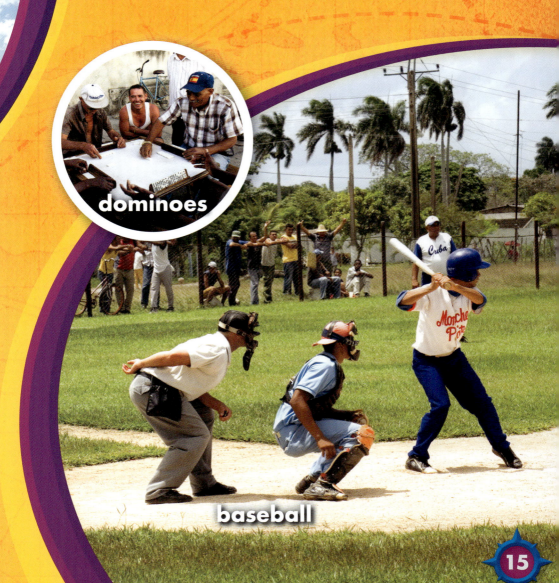

Moros y cristianos, or beans and rice, are **staples**. Cubans enjoy a vegetable stew called *ajiaco*.

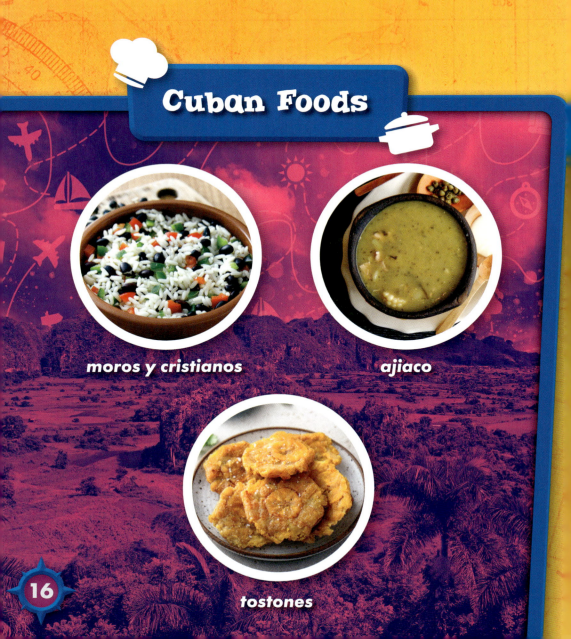

Cuban Foods

moros y cristianos

ajiaco

tostones

Tostones are fried plantains. They are served as a side dish.

Cuba's national holiday is Liberation Day. It is on January 1. There are parades, fireworks, and concerts.

In late July, Cubans enjoy Carnival. They dance and honor their **culture**!

Cuba Facts

Size:
42,803 square miles
(110,860 square kilometers)

Population:
11,008,112 (2022)

National Holiday:
Liberation Day (January 1)

Main Language:
Spanish

Capital City:
Havana

Famous Face

Name: José Abreu

Famous For: Major League Baseball player who has won MVP and many other awards

Religions

- other: 1%
- Christian: 59%
- none: 23%
- folk religion: 17%

Top Landmarks

Desembarco del Granma National Park

Parque Histórico Morro y Cabaña

Sierra Maestra

Glossary

ancestors—relatives who lived long ago

Christians—people who believe in the words of Jesus Christ

coral reefs—groups of corals that grow in warm, shallow ocean waters

culture—the beliefs, arts, and ways of life in a place or society

hurricanes—tropical storms with high winds, rain, thunder, and lightning

mangrove swamps—thick tropical forests that can grow along coasts in salty water

plains—large areas of flat land

staples—widely used foods or other items

tropical—related to a warm place near the equator

West Indies—the islands between southeastern North America and northern South America in the Caribbean Sea

To Learn More

AT THE LIBRARY

Kenney, Karen Latchana. *Rain Forests*. Minneapolis, Minn.: Bellwether Media, 2022.

Kenney, Karen Latchana. *Saving the Manatee*. Minneapolis, Minn.: Jump!, 2019.

Mattern, Joanne. *Cuba*. Minneapolis, Minn.: Jump!, 2019.

ON THE WEB

Factsurfer.com gives you a safe, fun way to find more information.

1. Go to www.factsurfer.com.
2. Enter "Cuba" into the search box and click 🔍.
3. Select your book cover to see a list of related content.

Index

animals, 10, 11
Atlantic Ocean, 4
baseball, 15
beaches, 6
capital (see Havana)
Caribbean Sea, 4
Carnival, 18, 19
Cave of Santo Tomás, 7
Christians, 12
coast, 6
coral reefs, 6
Cuba facts, 20–21
dance, 14, 18
dominoes, 15
food, 16, 17
Gulf of Mexico, 4
Havana, 4, 5
hurricanes, 9
island, 4
Liberation Day, 18

mangrove swamps, 6
map, 5
music, 14, 18
people, 12, 15
plains, 6
rivers, 10
say hello, 13
Sierra Maestra mountains, 7
Spanish, 12, 13
summer, 8, 9
West Indies, 4
winter, 8

The images in this book are reproduced through the courtesy of: yiannisscheidt, front cover; Kamira, front cover, pp. 18-19; Riderfoot, p. 3; Sean Pavone, pp. 4-5; Deatonphotos, p. 5; Rostislav Ageev, p. 6; Alexandre G. Rosa, pp. 6-7; KKulikov, pp. 8-9; Inspired By Maps, p. 9; Geza Farkas, pp. 10-11; Thierry Eidenweil, p. 11 (American manatee); Sergey Uryadnikov, pp. 11 (Cuban ground iguana), 22-23; Laura Romin & Larry Dalton/ Alamy, p. 11 (Waterhouse's leaf-nosed bat); Elliotte Rusty Harold, p. 11 (Cuban trogon); Karis48, p. 12; lisegagne, pp. 12-13; photosounds, pp. 14-15; Martchan, p. 15 (dominoes); Antony Souter/ Alamy, p. 15 (baseball); etorres, p. 16 (*moros y cristianos*); Ezume Images, p. 16 (*ajiaco*); Elena Veselova, p. 16 (*tostones*); Christian Schmidt/ Alamy, p. 17; carlos gonzalez ximenez, p. 18; titoOnz, p. 20 (flag); Koji Watanabe / Stringer/ Getty Images, p. 20 (José Abreu); rchphoto, p. 21 (*Desembarco del Granma* National Park); Studio MDF, p. 21 (*Parque Histórico Morro y Cabaña*); Christian Kaehler, p. 21 (Sierra Maestra).

24